Mojave
National Preserve

Mojave National Preserve is both vast and intimate. The product of hundreds of millions of years of geologic activity, its enormous valleys and isolated mountain ranges redefine our sense of space and time. In an ever shrinking world, here is a place where silence and solitude survive.

Snow-capped Granite Mountains peek over the Kelso Dunes.

Ultimately the desert rewards the patient, those who slow down and surrender to nature's rhythms. Take a walk or drive the backroads to discover a diverse and complex world of rare plants and animals and incomparable geology.

In years of good rainfall, the sheer beauty of the Mojave Desert can be stunning. Look out over the sloping valleys and the normally gray-brown desertscape takes on a green cast as long-dormant seeds sprout and annual grasses or wildflowers fill in the empty spaces between shrubs. Cholla, beavertail cactus, and the Mojave's signature plant, the Joshua tree, can put on spectacular floral displays, turning the desert into a garden busy with life.

Mojave National Preserve encompasses 1.6 million acres of diverse desert terrain, from flat dry lake beds (known as "playas") to stands of white fir nestled near its highest peaks. The park was created in 1994 as part of the California Desert Protection Act, one of the most comprehensive pieces of environmental legislation ever passed in the lower 48 states. The Mojave is managed by the National Park Service and is the service's third largest holding outside of Alaska.

"No false eyelashes, no cosmetics, no fancy clothes, just pure plain naked geology with a good coat of tan . . . "

Mojave National Preserve protects a critical section of the Mojave Desert, the smallest of the North American deserts. Nearly 300 species of animals, including desert bighorn sheep and the threatened desert tortoise, live here. Its human history takes in the full sweep of the American West: Native American cultures, early explorers, railroads, mining, and ranching.

Naked Geology

The sparseness of desert vegetation enables visitors to readily discern the forces that shaped and formed the Mojave Desert. As geologist and author Robert Sharp summed it up, "No false eyelashes, no cosmetics, no fancy clothes, just pure plain naked geology with a good coat of tan . . . " (By tan, he meant desert varnish, a dark, oxidized material high in iron and manganese that forms on rock.)

Several major faults helped define the Mojave's boundaries and ultimately its climate. About 25 million years ago, activity along the San Andreas Fault created the San Gabriel Mountains, and further north tectonic action uplifted the Sierra Nevada Range. Both block Pacific storms before they reach the Mojave, reducing rainfall and creating an arid environment.

California barrel cactus grows out of basalt that formed from a lava flow just 1,500 years ago.

In addition, twenty other major faults cross the Mojave. Most of them trend southeast to northwest and help form the area's Basin and Range topography, where narrow mountain ranges rise thousands of feet over intervening basins.

Many of its mountain ranges appear partially buried in their own debris. These sloping fields of sand, gravel, and boulders are known as alluvial fans and result from water and wind slowly wearing down the mountains. Narrow at the source and gracefully spreading as they flow downslope, alluvial fans often fill surrounding basins or converge with fans from neighboring canyons to form *bajadas*.

The forces of erosion have yielded dramatic results at two of the park's most compelling ranges: the New York Mountains and the Granite Mountains consist of broken granite rock, exposed by uplift. The remaining rock has formed an assortment of stacks and spires, beautiful both for their shapes and a rich, golden color that leaps out against the darker surrounding desert terrain.

In contrast, one of the park's most significant geologic landmarks is all but invisible to casual observers. Nearly symmetrical, the Cima Dome is 25 miles across and rises 1,500 feet above the surrounding basins, so gently that you could be on the surface and not even realize it. The dome, actually a granite formation known as monzonite, formed underground as molten rock cooled and hardened. Erosion gradually removed the overlying material and created the dome's contours.

Cima Dome is just one of many areas of the Mojave influenced by igneous activity. One of the park's most popular destinations is Hole-in-the-Wall, where hikers use metal rings set in the rock to lower themselves through a water-worn slot canyon, cut through a reddish wall of volcanic tuff deposited 17.8 million years ago.

Nor is the area's volcanism all the stuff of geologic time. Located north of Kelbaker Road, the Cinder Cones National Natural Landmark is a fractured, jagged basalt lava field (400 feet thick in places) with 30 cinder cones that show evidence of volcanic activity as recently as 1,500 years ago.

Indeed, while we sometimes think of geology as part of the distant past, in the Kelso Dunes you can literally see the land being shaped before your very eyes.

The 700-foot high Kelso Dunes are the third tallest in North America. Catch them at dawn or dusk, when the sun colors these sands in subtle shades of rose and violet and sharpens the scythe-like edges of the dune ridges.

The 65-square-mile dune field sits north of the Granite Mountains and at the southeast end of the 25-mile-long Devil's Playground, a sand-covered plain. Prevailing winds carry grains (mostly quartz and feldspar) from the Soda Dry Lake toward the dune field, where they accumulate thanks to crosswinds and mountain barriers.

While the dunes are evidence of the ongoing shaping of the land, the sand itself hints at a time when the Mojave was a more verdant place than the arid world we see today.

Within the last 1.6 million years, the region experienced times of wetter, cooler climate. During those times the Mojave River, rising in the San Bernardino Mountains, flowed frequently and carried a rich load of sediment into the now dry lake beds, such as Soda Lake. As these lakes periodically

TOP: Silver cholla is named for the way its spine catches the sunlight.
BOTTOM: The New York Mountains tower behind blooming Cooper golden bush.

dried, the sedimentary materials originally carried by the river were blown toward the Devil's Playground and eventually the dunes.

The same process continues today during the rare times that the Mojave actually flows. A curious river, the Mojave has been dubbed the "Upside-down River" for its contrarian ways: it's wider at its source than at its mouth, it doesn't flow into the ocean, and it primarily flows underground. However, in particularly wet years, water does flow across the desert floor and helps the dry lakes reemerge, if briefly, as genuine bodies of water.

High Desert Climate

Joshua trees can branch extensively depending on their genes as well as how much moisture and sunlight they receive.

Deserts are generally understood as areas where potential evaporation exceeds precipitation. The Mojave is one of four deserts in the American West that together form the third largest desert system in the world. Although elevations in the park range from 930 feet at Soda Lake to 7,829 feet atop

Clark Mountain, the Mojave as a whole is a high desert environment. The park itself constitutes an ecological meeting zone, mingling portions of the Great Basin and Sonoran Deserts within its boundaries.

Unlike the Sonoran Desert, which experiences two distinct rainy seasons, the Mojave receives most of its scant precipitation during winter storms. Thanks to the high elevation, visitors sometimes bear witness to an unusual event: Joshua trees covered by snow.

Temperature varies considerably with elevation. During July, the year's hottest month, temperatures at 4,200-foot Granite Mountain average a comfortable 90 degrees. At Zzyzx, where the elevation is a mere 930-feet, the average temperature soars to 109.

While the Mojave is justly famous for its summer heat, for six months of the year temperatures remain dependably in a moderate range well below 90 degrees—even at its hottest spots. On triple-digit summer days, the desert's lack of cloud cover means that the daytime heat quickly radiates back toward the sky after nightfall. Daily summer temperature variations are routinely more than 30 degrees, creating gorgeous, balmy nights. On occasion, temperatures vary 80 degrees in a single day.

The Mojave sits in the rain shadow created by the tall mountains that form its western and southern boundaries. However, just as with temperature, elevation plays a critical role for precipitation; Granite Mountain, for example, receives an annual average of 8.5 inches of rain, more than double Zzyzx's 3.35 inches.

When it comes to precipitation, "average" tends to be a deceptive term because Mojave rainfall is rarely consistent from year-to-year. The former town of Bagdad, just south of the park, owns the distinction of having endured the longest period without rain of any spot in the United States: 767 days from October 3, 1912 to November 8, 1914. In other years, plentiful rains cause an explosion of spring wildflowers.

Vegetation and Habitats

Variations in temperature and rainfall, combined with the diversity of soil types found in the Mojave, allow a wide range of plant communities to thrive here. About one-fourth of the Mojave Desert's plant species grow nowhere else in the world.

Mojave's most barren places are its dry lake beds, where a high alkaline content prevents all but the most salt-tolerant plants from growing. Even the creosote bush, which grows over 75 percent of the Mojave and is the most widely distributed of the park's plants, is unable to withstand these conditions.

The creosote's success across the remainder of the Mojave is a study in water conservation techniques. During extended drought periods, creosote will drop many of its mature leaves, even whole branches. When rains do

TOP: Barrel cactus, desert globemallow, and banana yucca above Lanfair Valley during sunrise.
BOTTOM: The magenta bloom of beavertail prickly pear cactus attracts pollinators.

FROM TOP TO BOTTOM: Just part of the plentiful life of the Mojave Desert: Scott's oriole, kit fox, jackrabbit, kangaroo rat, leopard lizard.

come, however, creosote can quickly leaf out and sprout small and fragrant yellow flowers.

With their extensive root systems (up to 50 feet in length), individual creosote tap into virtually all the available moisture in their immediate area. That leads creosote to grow in evenly spaced vast stands that can spread for miles.

The species' mastery of the harsh desert environment is also evident in its lifespan. Creosote grow from a central root crown, and as the stems nearest the crown die, fresh branches spring up away from the center to form new shrubs. Scientists have estimated that one creosote ring southwest of Mojave National Preserve dates to 11,700 years ago.

For all its superlatives, the shrubby creosote lacks the charisma of the Mojave's most celebrated plant, the Joshua tree. While the Joshua tree ranges into the Great Basin and Sonoran Deserts, it has become synonymous with the Mojave. There are two different subspecies of Joshua trees: the larger *Yucca brevifolia brevifolia,* which grows at Joshua Tree National Park, and the more densely branched *Yucca brevifolia jaegeriana,* found in the park and other areas of the eastern Mojave.

The Joshua tree, actually a member of the lily family, has a woody trunk and twisting branches with dagger-like leaves growing from their ends. When the leaves die, they dry and form what is known as a "shag" on branches and the trunk, adding to the Joshua tree's grizzled appearance.

The branches earned the plant its biblical name from Mormon pioneers, who thought the bent and twisting limbs recalled the upraised arms of Joshua as he urged his followers to the Promised Land. In contrast, explorer John C. Fremont called them "the most repulsive tree in the vegetable kingdom." Perhaps Fremont never saw Joshua trees in bloom, when clusters of densely packed, six-petaled cream and pale green flowers spring from the branch tips.

Joshua trees primarily grow at elevations from 2,000 to 6,000 feet and prefer fairly level, well-drained terrain. In many places, you can literally see the transition zone where just a few scattered Joshuas begin to grow among stands of creosote before density increases further up slope, and the trees form full-fledged forests. Magnificent stands prosper in the Lanfair Valley, while the Joshua trees on Cima Dome have earned acclaim as the world's most dense Joshua forest.

Joshua trees themselves can be huge, towering 30 to 40 feet above the surrounding vegetation. Like many things in the Mojave, they are a study in patience, sometimes growing only two to four inches per year. Not surprisingly, therefore, Joshua trees are long lived. Typical life span is about 150 years, although botanists have estimated that individual trees have lived 500 years or more.

For all the Joshua tree's associations with its home desert, it is a smaller and less spectacular yucca that actually bears the Mojave moniker. With their sharp, narrow leaves, the Mojave yucca superficially resemble Joshua trees, especially younger Joshua trees that have yet to grow branches off their trunks. The Mojave yucca (also known as Spanish dagger) grows in many of the same lower elevation areas as Joshua trees.

Not all of the park's plant communities have such a stereotypically prickly and spiny desert character. As you gain elevation, Joshua tree stands begin to thin and you enter the realm of the piñon-juniper woodland. This community of drought resistant, cone-bearing small trees and sagebrush prospers between 5,000–8,000-foot elevations; the Mid Hills area offers some of the park's best piñon-juniper habitat.

Throughout the park, isolated pockets of plant communities endure from the days when the Mojave was a cooler and wetter place. At Caruthers Canyon in the New York Mountains, stands of chaparral include plants such as California lilac *(ceanothus)* and oak endure more than 100 miles from their prime turf. Piute Creek, a perennial stream in the eastern part of the park, hosts a riparian forest of cottonwood and willow. Just yards away on adjacent slopes, nothing larger than cacti can grow. In scattered places in the Providence Mountains and at Clark Mountain, even a few fern species, such as the maidenhair, persist in the Mojave — just about the last region you would expect to find them.

Animal Life

Fossil evidence shows that during more temperate times, the Mojave supported a menagerie that is all but unimaginable in today's hot and dry environment. Large mammals, including saber-toothed cats, horses, giant sloths, and mastodons, all roamed the area.

That said, Mojave still supports a surprisingly diverse assortment of animals. One of the rarest species in the park is the endangered Mohave tui chub, a native fish now limited to Lake Tuendae, a spring-fed manmade pond at the Desert Studies Center at Zzyzx, and a few other ponds in the Mojave Desert.

In many instances, the life cycles of native plants and animals are intricately linked. Not surprisingly, the most fascinating and complex interactions center on Joshua trees.

Joshua trees and yucca moths live in a mutually dependent relationship: the plant provides food and shelter for the moth's larvae, and the adult moths help propagate the Joshua trees by pollinating its flowers. As female yucca moths move about the clusters to deposit eggs, pollen collects on their heads and is eventually delivered to blossoms on other Joshua trees. When the young hatch, they live inside the tree's fruit and eat some but not all of its seeds.

For the night lizard, the Joshua tree provides all the basics for survival. The lizard lives under downed trees and branches or underneath the debris that collects at its base, protected both from predators and the heat and sun. The debris also plays host to crickets, termites, and other bugs on which the lizard feeds.

The Desert Tortoise

The desert tortoise embodies the contradictions of the Mojave itself: tough yet fragile, ancient but vulnerable to the forces of modernity.

The tortoise lives in sand or gravel terrain, primarily within creosote scrub. It is most active during rainy spells, when annual grasses, forbs, and puddles are available. During these periods, the tortoise's weight may increase by more than 40 percent. During rainless stretches and the cold winter months, however, the tortoise will remain in its burrow, slowing its metabolism while dormant.

Overall, the desert tortoise is a remarkable success story: individuals can live 80 years and the species has survived for millions of years. But the tortoise faces threats that have led to a precipitous population decline: loss of habitat due to development, disease borne by released captive tortoises, predation by ravens (whose numbers have grown because of increased trash in the desert), crushing by off-road vehicles, and loss of forage to grazing animals.

TOP: Bighorn sheep
RIGHT: The Castle Peaks Hiking
Corridor takes visitors to the top
of the Castle Mountains in the
eastern part of the Preserve.

Within the Joshua tree forest and across its other habitats, the Mojave lives up to the desert's popular reputation as a haven for reptiles. Mojave rattlesnakes, chuckwallas, iguanas, and desert horned lizards all thrive here. The most celebrated of the park's reptiles, the desert tortoise, is now a federally listed threatened species.

While reptiles are hardly unexpected, many visitors are surprised to discover the desert's rich assortment of resident and seasonal birds. An estimated twenty-five bird species nest in Joshua trees alone.

With its black head and striking yellow coloring, the Scott's oriole is one of the Mojave's most beautiful birds; its lilting call provides a sweet counter-point to the often silent desert. These birds, which migrate from Mexico in spring, build hanging nests made from Joshua tree fibers underneath the tree's jagged and protective leaf clusters. In contrast, hawks and other raptors nest on the tops of branches, a convenient vantage point for hunting the assorted rodents who live in the Joshua tree forest.

Desert rodents, including kangaroo rats, antelope ground squirrels, and jackrabbits, have adapted well to their arid environment. One of the simplest strategies is to remain underground in their relatively moist and cool burrows during the heat of day, then emerge at night to forage. But these animals also display physiological adaptations to help them cope with heat and aridity.

Amazingly, the kangaroo rat can go its entire life without ever drinking water. Instead, it derives its moisture from the breakdown of seeds and other foods that it eats.

Several larger mammals make their home in the desert. Coyotes are a common sight throughout the Mojave, while kit and gray foxes are less numerous and tend to be active at night. Mountain lions and bobcats are even rarer still.

Of the larger herbivores, you're most likely to see mule deer, especially in higher elevation areas. With their magnificent spiral horns, desert bighorn sheep are perhaps the most majestic of the Mojave's mammals. Difficult to spot, these herd animals prefer rugged mountains where they display amazing agility across the steep and precarious terrain.

Like the kangaroo rat, the 100–200 pound desert bighorn makes efficient use of its limited resources. The sheep's slow-working digestive process allows it to feed on even nutrient-deficient plants. In winter they get almost all their water from green plants, but in summer they must rely on scattered desert watering holes.

Humans in the Desert

Human beings have lived in, and ranged through, the Mojave Desert for the past 12,000 years or more. The earliest occupants inhabited the region during times of higher precipitation, when the dry lakes we see today were actual bodies of water. Researchers have found an assortment of stone tools along the

one-time shorelines of these lakes and at rock shelters near mountain springs.

Even as the climate became more arid and game populations declined, humans remained in the Mojave. In historic times, two main Native American groups lived in and around the park: the Mojave, who occupied areas along the Colorado River, and the Chemehuevi, a nomadic people who migrated into the area about 900 years ago.

The Mojave and the Chemehuevi come from separate language traditions and led vastly different lives. The Chemehuevi, a Paiute people related to the Native Americans of the Great Basin, were hunter-gatherers who relied on the resources of the desert, living off small game, fruit from cacti, and assorted seeds. They crafted baskets made of willow, rushes, and devil's claw, and created some of the petroglyphs in the Mojave.

The Mojave are a Yuman-speaking tribe, part of a family linked by a common language, that lives in the deserts of Southern California and Arizona. Making use of seasonal flooding along the Colorado River, they cultivated crops including corn, beans, and melons.

The Mojave were also great travelers; they traded with tribes in the interior Southwest and those nearly 300 miles west on the Pacific Coast. They also established a network of trails westward across the desert, including along the course of the Mojave River, that would serve as routes for the first Europeans who ventured into the area.

The Franciscan priest Francisco Garcés followed Native American trails during his 1776 explorations. The Mojave helped guide him as far west as the Mission San Gabriel.

In 1826, the famed trapper and explorer Jedediah Strong Smith became the first European-American to journey across the Mojave Desert, using the route that would become the Mojave Road. The brutal daytime heat forced his party to travel mostly at night.

As explorations of California increased, other Western legends also used this route. In 1829–30 Kit Carson crossed the Mojave, and in 1844 John C. Fremont followed it eastward after surveying the Oregon Trail and the Sierra Nevada. During the 1850s the Mojave road became the mail route under the protection of the U.S. Army.

The railroad reached the Mojave Desert at Needles in 1883 and a short line, the Nevada Southern, began operating in the Lanfair Valley area of the park in 1893. The railroad's arrival helped connect the Mojave Desert more directly to the outside world, thus accelerating economic development in the desert. Mining operations, which had started in the area in the 1860s, now had a more cost-effective way to transport ore.

The start of mining operations, and with it the growing desert population, spurred cattle ranching, which also benefited from the railroad. The Rock Springs Land & Cattle Company grew into a huge operation with 10,000 cattle spread out over one million acres.

TOP: Nineteenth-century residents of Manvel enjoy an outing.
BOTTOM: A beautifully woven Chemehuevi basket